_S_PORTS GREAT
GRANT HILL

BASKETBALL

For Other *Sports Great Books* call:
(800) 398-2504

GRANT HILL

John Albert Torres

—SPORTS GREAT BOOKS—

Enslow Publishers, Inc.

40 Industrial Road   PO Box 38
Box 398   Aldershot
Berkeley Heights, NJ   07922   Hants GU12 6BP
USA   UK

http://www.enslow.com

Library of Congress Cataloging-in-Publication Data

Torres, John Albert.
    Sports great Grant Hill / John Albert Torres.
        p. cm. — (Sports great books)
    Includes index.
    Summary: Examines the life of basketball star, Grant Hill, from his childhood
in Virginia, through his years at Duke University, to his professional career with
the Detroit Pistons.
    ISBN 0-7660-1467-3
    1. Hill, Grant—Juvenile literature. 2. Basketball players—United States—
Biography—Juvenile literature. [1. Hill, Grant. 2. Basketball players.
3. Afro-Americans—Biography] I. Title. II. Series.
GV884.H45 T67 2001
796.323'092—dc21

                          00-008397

Printed in the United States of America

10 9 8 7 6 5 4 3 2 1

To Our Readers: All Internet Addresses in this book were active and appropriate when
we went to press. Any comments or suggestions can be sent by e-mail to
Comments@enslow.com or to the address on the back cover.

Illustration Credits: Barry Gossage/NBA Photos, p. 53; David Sherman/NBA
Photos, pp. 9, 45; Fernando Medina/NBA Photos, p. 55; Frank McGrath/NBA
Photos, p. 47; Gary Dineen/NBA Photos, pp. 39, 41; Glenn James/NBA
Photos, p. 22; Greg Shamus/NBA Photos, p. 49; Jeff Reinking/NBA Photos,
pp. 26, 35; Jon Hayt/NBA Photos, p. 11; Nathaniel S. Butler/NBA Photos, pp.
16, 19; Noren Trotman/NBA Photos, p. 21; Scott Cunningham/NBA Photos,
pp. 28, 37, 58; Tim Mantoani/NBA Photos, pp. 13, 30.

Cover Illustration: Sam Forencich/NBA Photos.

Contents

One-Man Wrecking Crew

Grant Hill, superstar forward for the National Basketball Association's (NBA) Detroit Pistons, was in the middle of a special game. The date was February 8, 1999. It seemed as if the basket was much wider for him than usual, and every shot he threw up toward the basket went in. He was scoring at will, driving to the basket, taking long jumpers, and drawing fouls. Grant Hill was doing it all. Yet, as is often the case when there is a superstar player on a mediocre team, the Pistons were having a tough time putting away the pesky Washington Wizards.

In fact, Washington guard Rod Strickland drove the lane untouched and banked in a running one-hander with 14.5 seconds left in the game. Washington had the lead, 103–102. It seemed as if another great Grant Hill performance would be wasted.

Grant Hill dribbled the ball across the midcourt line and thought of calling a timeout to let the offense regroup. But then he looked up at the defense and saw something that probably no one else in the building could see—an inch of daylight.

He drove left toward the baseline as the game clock neared the ten-second point. Hill faked a move toward his left and then cut back down the baseline. Suddenly, in a blink of an eye, Hill was exploding toward the basket for a seemingly game-winning slam dunk. Washington's all-star power forward, Juwan Howard, could do nothing but grab Hill and commit a foul.

"I started to call timeout and then I just decided to see what they would do," Hill said. "In retrospect, calling time-out would have been the smart thing to do—but it worked."

Hill calmly walked to the free-throw line and sank both shots, to give the Pistons a 104–103 lead. The two points were Grant's 45th and 46th points of the game—a career high!

The fans who had packed The Palace of Auburn Hills to watch their favorite player dominate the game rose and gave him a standing ovation. Hill acknowledged their cheers, but he knew the game was not over yet. The Wizards had about ten seconds left to win the game. Now Hill focused his mind on defense, stopping the other team from scoring. The fans continued their ovation, but they should have waited. The best was yet to come.

A few seconds later, with Washington desperate for a bucket, Tim Legler somehow broke free of the defense and caught a pass in three-point territory. All alone, Legler squared up to hoist the potential game-winner. But here was Grant Hill again, making a tremendous play. He rushed out at Legler, hoping to cause him to change his shot. But Hill's incredible quickness and long arms actually allowed him to deflect the shot just as the buzzer sounded. The Pistons had won the game. This was especially important during the strike-shortened 1999 NBA season. The regular-season schedule was cut down from eighty-two games to fifty, so every victory meant that much more.

Hill had shot 14-for-21 from the field, connected on 18 of 22 free throws, passed for 7 assists, pulled down 7

Grant Hill is not afraid to take on three defenders, as he is doing here against the Minnesota Timberwolves.

rebounds, stole the ball twice, and blocked 2 shots. Talk about a one-man wrecking crew!

It was just another amazing night from the man who is adored in Detroit and respected throughout the league. In fact, many people regard him as being capable of filling some awfully big shoes. Some say that Grant Hill can replace the legendary Michael Jordan as the NBA's next all-time great.

The ultimate team player, Hill would much rather see his team start winning on a more consistent basis than be heralded as the next Jordan.

Even before Jordan retired from professional basketball, some were already proclaiming Hill as the heir apparent. It is something that Grant Hill is not entirely comfortable with. "People are so eager for a next Jordan," Hill said, "they tried to place it on me, or Kobe [Bryant], or Penny [Hardaway]. I say let him retire and someone will emerge. I've decided I'm just going to be me." That "me" has turned out to be a superstar NBA player.

After that 46-point performance against Washington, Hill turned in one of his best seasons ever. In one game, on April 7, Hill caught fire in the fourth quarter as he scored 15 of his 30 points against the Atlanta Hawks leading his team to a come-from-behind victory. For the season, he led the Pistons in several categories, including scoring an average of 21.1 points, 7.1 rebounds, and 6.0 assists per game. He was named to the All-NBA second team and was named the Player of the Week on May 2. Because of the strike-shortened season, no NBA All-Star Game was held. If there had been one, Hill surely would have been named a starter. He led his team to a respectable 29–21 record and, more important, a berth in the playoffs. The Pistons had missed the playoffs the previous year.

Unfortunately, the Piston's first-round opponent was

Hill, who is respected throughout the league, throwing one down over Miami center Alonzo Mourning.

the tough veteran Atlanta Hawks team, led by Dikembe Mutombo and Steve Smith.

The Hawks dominated the first two games of the best-of-five series with victories in Atlanta. But the series took on a different look when it moved to Detroit for two games. Detroit took Game 3, 79–63, and then the Auburn Hills crowd was raring for the Pistons to even the series.

Hill made sure of that. He scored 23 points as the Pistons blew out the Hawks, 103–82, to tie the series. In one sequence, while the game was still close, Hill poked an Atlanta pass away, picked up the loose ball, and raced upcourt. The only thing in his way was Atlanta center and shot-blocking expert Dikembe Mutombo, who is known to stop fast breaks even before they start. Hill drove right at the seven-footer, gave him a ball fake, and then elevated over him for a thunderous slam dunk. The crowd went wild. That play, along with another steal and fast break a few seconds later, catapulted the Pistons to the home-court victory.

The Pistons dropped the next game in Atlanta, 87–75, and their season was over. Hill led the team by scoring 19.4 points in the five games. In the final game of the series he scored 21 points, grabbed 7 rebounds, and dished out 11 assists, but it was not enough.

During his five seasons in the NBA, Grant Hill has established himself as a rare superstar. He is the player who does not actively seek out the limelight. As with Michael Jordan, the spotlight seems to find him—and rarely will Grant Hill disappoint. Hill has accomplished more in his five seasons than most players do in their entire careers. The one thing that has eluded him, however, and the main thing that separates most players from Michael Jordan-like status, is a championship. Hill would like nothing more than to help hoist a championship banner.

Grant Hill is not quite the next Michael Jordan—yet.

Grant Hill's clean-cut image off the court, and hard-nosed style of play on the floor make him an excellent role model.

But his soft-spoken image, his clean-cut style of play, and the way he shoots the basketball have helped put him among the league's leading vote-getters for All-Star Games and Most Valuable Player votes. He is one of the most popular players in the game today.

"I've often wondered why and how things have gone the way they have, and how I was able to get the most votes for the All-Star Game the last two years," Hill said. "It truly amazes me." When asked about the origin of his popularity, he said, "Honestly, I don't know."

What Grant Hill does know, however, is that he had an upbringing unlike that of most of his peers in the NBA. He also knows that his career started on the afternoon when he fell in love with sports. A few years later he would fall in love with the game of basketball.

Chapter 2

Natural Athlete

Most kids who love sports pretend that their fathers or mothers are professional athletes and not post office workers, nurses, truck drivers, or homemakers. Most kids wish that their dads were blasting home runs for the New York Yankees, or slam-dunking basketballs for the Los Angeles Lakers, or running for touchdowns for the Dallas Cowboys. For Grant Hill, that wish was not a dream. It was a reality.

Grant Henry Hill was born on October 5, 1972, the son of high-powered attorney Janet Hill and Dallas Cowboys superstar running back Calvin Hill. Calvin was known as a thinking man's running back. He was a superior athlete who relied more on his wits, strategy, and knowledge of the game than on his also remarkable athleticism. In fact, Calvin Hill became the first Cowboys running back to gain 1,000 yards in a single season. He was great even before the world heard of such other great Cowboys as Tony Dorsett and Emmitt Smith. Calvin led the Cowboys to their first Super Bowl victory.

Calvin and Janet met after a Harvard-Yale college football game in 1968. Calvin was the star running back for Yale, while Janet was an honor student at the exclusive school. Two years later they were married. Two years after

With his explosive first step, Grant Hill moves past Gary Payton of the Seattle SuperSonics. Hill may have gotten his quickness from his father, Calvin, a former NFL running back.

that, Grant was born—the only child of two people who were also only children.

Grant was born in Dallas, Texas. He lived for a while in Hawaii, but was mainly raised in Reston, Virginia, after his father changed uniforms and played for the Washington Redskins.

Grant's parents wanted the best for their only child, so they stressed the importance of the finer things in life. They enrolled Grant in the best schools, gave him piano and art lessons, and monitored who he chose as friends. His father, who knew what it took to succeed, constantly lectured Grant about commitment and mental toughness. His mother, who was known in the Hill household as The General, supplied Grant with long lists of rules and punishments.

While being the son of a successful lawyer and a football hero certainly had clear benefits, there were some, including the future basketball star himself, who thought Grant's parents were too hard on him. "They were too strict, if you ask me," said Grant. "I didn't make any mistakes as a kid because I couldn't. I tried to negotiate with them but they were too smart for me."

Janet Hill stressed to her son that not many athletes get to make it on a professional level. She wanted him to concentrate first and foremost on his studies. That was always the number one priority. Sports came second.

"Our culture's emphasis on sports . . . gives kids an unrealistic expectation of the amount of brains necessary to be excellent at athletics," she said. "It would be a big, big mistake to think the best player in basketball, Michael Jordan, is not a smart man. There is no way he could have achieved the level of excellence he has achieved if he were not intelligent. You've never seen a championship team in any sport led by a dumb person."

Janet Hill was a college dormmate with Hillary

Rodham Clinton, the future First Lady. Janet Hill would later build a successful consulting firm with Clifford Alexander, the former Secretary of the Army.

Janet Hill even went so far as to contact the National Association of High School Principals to find out the odds of high school basketball players' making it into the NBA. She wanted not to discourage Grant but to show him the reality, so he would know just how difficult it would be to make it into professional basketball. According to *USA Weekend*, each year there are about 250,000 high school varsity basketball players, 4,700 NCAA Division I basketball players, and only 60 new NBA players! Those odds are staggering.

Unlike many of today's basketball stars, Grant grew up in a big house with a stable family. He got to travel all around the world and meet a lot of famous people. It certainly was not your average childhood. One of the famous people that Grant met and admired was Roger Staubach, the starting quarterback for the Dallas Cowboys, who was Calvin Hill's best friend.

Grant wanted to be a star quarterback too. He would often ask his dad if he could play for the local children's football league. But that turned out to be one rule Grant could never break. His father would not allow Grant to play football until high school. He explained that he did not want Grant to be compared to his dad in every play, every game, from an early age.

Sometimes Grant was not comfortable with being the son of a famous dad. He would not tell people who his father was, unless they asked him directly. One time, when Calvin Hill came to speak at Grant's school, Grant faked a stomachache and stayed in the nurse's office the entire time. Whenever his parents would pick him up from school, Grant insisted they use the old Volkswagen, instead of their new Porsche and Mercedes luxury cars.

Hill says that his parents were strict. His mother made it clear to Grant that his studies were his priority, and his father did not want him to play football.

"I've always just wanted to blend in and be like everybody else," Grant said. "I didn't want anybody, especially my friends, thinking I was better than them. I just wanted to be a down to earth guy and have my own identity."

When Grant was growing up, two of his idols were famous African-American athletes. He loved to watch basketball star Julius Erving (Doctor J) and tennis ace Arthur Ashe. Grant did not like them simply because they were great athletes. He liked them because they also set a good example for kids. They set high standards and took on the responsibility of being positive role models, which some athletes today avoid. He also liked the fact that they were African Americans, like him. The class and grace of Erving and Ashe influence Grant even today.

Although he was not allowed to play football, that did not mean Grant was not allowed to play sports. In fact, he excelled in soccer and, of course, basketball. He joined several soccer leagues and won many trophies. He was, and still is, a natural athlete. His tall, thin frame made him a natural on the vast soccer fields. They also made him a natural in the driveway, the schoolyard, or the gym—anywhere that there was a basketball hoop. When Grant turned thirteen, he grew a few inches, and just simply fell in love with the game of basketball. It was not that the game was new to him, but suddenly now he was pretty good at it. He joined the local Amateur Athletic Union (AAU) youth basketball team and became its star.

During that time, Grant and his family had season tickets for the Georgetown University men's basketball team. They would make the trip for every game. It was a good way for the family to spend some quality time together, and it was also a good way for Grant to learn the nuances, the real strategy of winning basketball.

Today, Grant credits a lot of people for the wonderful upbringing he enjoyed. He said it would be nearly

Flying through the air, Hill converts an easy basket. From a young age, it was clear that Hill was a natural athlete.

As a teenager, Grant Hill got the chance to travel and play basketball in AAU tournaments. One year his team won the tournament championship, beating a team from Detroit, a place that Hill came to know very well.

impossible to credit just one person with his development as a person, but it is obvious that his parents played the most important role.

Although he was raised in a strict household, Grant was also raised with a lot of love and affection. Calvin and Janet Hill surrounded Grant with people who truly cared for their son and who would look out for them. "My parents certainly showed me the value of hard work," Grant said.

There was one specific moment while he was growing up that planted the seed of greatness in basketball into Grant's mind. His AAU team was set to face a team from Detroit, a team of tough, inner-city kids, that included players like Chris Webber and Jalen Rose—two of today's NBA stars.

Grant simply dominated the game with his quickness, his shooting, his tenacity—and his smarts. He grabbed rebounds, dove for loose balls, and left the team from Detroit wondering just who this Grant Hill was. He was named to the AAU all-tournament team, and his team won the championship. When Grant got home, his father challenged him to a game of one-on-one basketball. It was the first time that Calvin really played hard against his son, trying to test just how good Grant was. He was not trying to burst his son's bubble; it was just that Calvin himself wondered how good his son really was.

Grant was already six-foot three-inches tall and was sure he could beat his thirty-eight-year-old father, who was still in great football shape. They played two games; the first to score eleven baskets would win. Grant dominated, just as he had against the Detroit team, and he won both games easily. From that moment on he decided to give up playing soccer. Now he was focused.

Chapter 3

High School Star

By the time Grant Hill was in his early teens, the local high school basketball coach had already heard about the player who dominated AAU games and was also the son of a great football player. Maybe the coach would get lucky and finally be able to coach a great one.

Grant and his father, Calvin Hill, often joked about the passing down of genes. Calvin often kidded his only son by telling him that since he only inherited half of his genes, then he would only be half the athlete that Calvin was. Grant would always look at his smirking dad and just break down laughing.

When Grant enrolled as a freshman at South Lakes High School in Reston, Virginia, he was taller than any other freshman and, as always, a step ahead of the crowd. He was ahead of others, even when he did not want to be.

Grant signed up for tryouts for the freshman basketball team and was looking forward to being part of a team with a few of his friends and other kids his age. But when he arrived at tryouts, the varsity head coach invited Grant to try out for the varsity team. He wanted Grant to skip the freshman and junior varsity levels and play with kids who were at least three years older than he was. Coach Wendell Byrd thought Grant would be happy. Instead, he saw the fourteen-year-old break down and cry. The coach tried talking to Grant, who was too upset to listen. "I didn't want to jump over my friends," Grant remembered. "I just wanted to be liked. I didn't want to seem better than anybody else."

Grant was still just a kid at heart. He did not want to feel rushed. He just wanted to be with his friends.

Coach Byrd did not give up. He pulled Grant to the side and read him the names of the players on the varsity team. When he was done with the list, Byrd asked Grant if he felt he was better than those guys. Grant said he was. Byrd told him to go home and talk with his family. He told Grant that he would be wasting quite an opportunity and a lot of valuable experience if he did not play varsity right away.

After a lot of talking with his family and a lot of thinking on his own, Grant recognized the opportunity that was being offered to him. He went back to school the next day and accepted the offer. Grant made the varsity team easily. He was a ninth-grader playing with kids just about ready for college.

Even though he was not a starting player, Grant learned a lot by playing with players so much older than he was. He worked hard in practice and earned enough playing time to average 10 points a game. More important, Grant began believing in himself. He began believing that he belonged at this level even if everyone else was older than he was. That boost to his confidence made him more committed to basketball than ever before.

During the off-season, Grant wanted to learn more about basketball. Oh sure, he could play it, and he was good, too. But now, Grant really wanted to learn what the

Knifing through the lane, Hill tries to make a play on Vin Baker of the Seattle SuperSonics.

game was about. The best way for him to do this, he thought, was by watching it. Grant soon began taping every basketball game he could with his VCR and even brought a video camera with him to the Georgetown games, which he still attended with his mother and father. Grant would tape every moment of every game and then go home, rewind the tape, and watch the game again. He began analyzing strategies, defenses, and moves to the basket. He became such a video nut that he actually broke five remote controls in one summer! He was especially interested in the NCAA 1982 championship game between Georgetown and North Carolina. "I've seen that game so many times that I know each and every move by heart," Grant said.

But unlike other kids his age, Grant was not interested in rewinding the tape to watch a slam dunk or a three-point bucket. He was more interested in watching the great passes, or the picks or screens that an offensive player would set. Grant loved to watch the team play together as a unit. He was enamored with the team concept of basketball. He relished the extra pass or the player who dove for the loose ball, or the smaller player who would suck it up and take a charge. He also loved to watch what guys did on the court without the ball. He began to realize that in basketball, much as in soccer, positioning was just as important for the players without the ball as it was for the one player who had it.

Grant would often watch those tapes with his boyhood friend Michael Ellison, who later worked in public relations for sports leagues and agencies. "Sometimes it was a tape we hadn't seen before, and he would just try to anticipate along with it," Ellison said. "It was amazing what he saw at that age."

Like a lot of other great players over the years, Grant developed a court sense. He would see the game through the eyes of the point guard. He anticipated every pass,

Hill lays up the finger-roll in front of former Georgetown center Dikembe Mutombo. Hill began to learn about the nuances and strategy of basketball by going to Georgetown basketball games when he was a teenager.

knew where every person on the court should be, and then learned how to break down a defense as an offensive player. Grant learned how to set picks, when to set up for a screen, and how to get around those obstacles while playing defense. He developed court vision, the ability to see everything on the basketball court as it should be.

Grant would spend hours watching tapes and then he would run out of the house, basketball in hand, so he could try out what he had just seen on the basketball court. "I couldn't wait to get on the court and recreate from memory a move I just saw," Grant said.

The hard work and video-watching really paid off for Grant during his sophomore year at South Lakes High School. He earned a starting position on the team and responded by averaging a team-high 25 points a game.

The next year Grant gave up some of the scoring in order to give the rest of his team more of a chance to win. He wanted to get some of the other players involved. His scoring dipped to 17 points a game when he was a junior, which did not make his father happy.

Calvin wanted Grant to attract enough attention to gain a college scholarship. He admired his son for his true team leadership and team play, but he thought that Grant could also help his team by scoring more points.

The next year, after a summer of watching videotapes and practicing, Grant dominated the high school league by averaging 30 points a game. He led the team to a winning record and a good run in the local high school tournament. But dominating on the basketball court was not the only excellence Grant was showing. He was an all-star in the classroom as well. Grant took his studies seriously and was an A-plus student.

For graduation, Grant earned the honor of class valedictorian, held for the student with the best grades in

As a senior in high school, Grant averaged 30 points per game, and also excelled in the classroom. As he entered college, he was unsure about what type of career he wanted to pursue.

the graduating class. It also gave Grant a chance to speak in front of his peers at the high school graduation.

Grant's parents were very proud of having raised a son that excelled in sports and in the classroom. "My husband and I were both nerdy 'A' students," Janet Hill said, laughing. "We set the bar high for Grant but we also understood that every child is different. If Grant's best is a 'B,' then it's not fair to require an 'A.' You have to put athletics second to your studies."

Even though Grant was great in basketball, and even though just about every major college in the country was trying to recruit him, he still was not sure what he wanted to do with his life. He loved the game of basketball but was not quite sure that he wanted to become a professional athlete. As the son of a professional athlete, he knew about both the positive and the negative. He remembered missing his father when Calvin Hill went on the road with his team. He also remembered the terrible amount of pressure he had to live up to as Calvin Hill's son.

Certainly he would play college basketball, but Grant also loved learning. Maybe a teaching career was in his future. Grant sometimes envisioned himself as a history teacher, helping others to learn what he already knew.

Because of his academic excellence and his athletic prowess, Grant had his pick of colleges and universities. His mother wanted him to go to Georgetown University and play basketball for longtime coach John Thompson. His dad wanted his son to go to the University of North Carolina and play for the legendary Dean Smith.

But, maybe for the first time in his life, Grant decided to go against his parents' wishes and chose to go where his heart led him. Grant announced that he would be attending Duke University and playing basketball there, with the Blue Devils.

Chapter 4

Reluctant Superstar

Duke University, a beautiful and historical learning institution in North Carolina, has long been considered a hotbed for basketball. It has a steady and well-coached program, and many of the country's top high school basketball players want to play for Duke. They want to be part of the Blue Devils' winning tradition.

Although it had never won the NCAA men's basketball championship, Duke was usually in the tournament and usually went deep into the very competitive championship contests. In fact, between 1963 and 1991 Duke finished in the prestigious Final Four a total of eight times. The Final Four is made up of the four teams, each of which wins its regional bracket of the tournament.

With Coach Mike Krzyzewski leading the way, and some excellent recruits including the likes of Christian Laettner, Brian Davis, and Bobby Hurley, the team had an excellent chance of returning to the Final Four.

Grant Hill, who had been named Northern Virginia's Player of the Year three times in high school, just may have been the final piece to the championship puzzle. Armed with the confidence that came with such a successful high school career, Hill was not the least bit intimidated the first time he stepped onto the court with his new teammates.

However, Hill is naturally shy, and he stayed away from the spotlight as he just tried to fit in with his new team.

His freshman season started out well. Hill was not yet a starter on the team, but he was very valuable to the team as the sixth man. This is a position held by the player who is the first man off the bench to make a substitution. Hill got a lot of playing time and did very well. Unlike other highly touted freshman who might be looking to impress, he did not shoot all the time. His goal was to make his team better, even if it meant a lower scoring average but more passing and rebounding on his part.

After one game, Hill was approached by NBA player Johnny Dawkins, who had been a superstar guard while he played for Duke. Dawkins was impressed when he watched Hill play. He asked the freshman who he thought was the best player on the team. Looking down, Hill said it was Christian Laettner. Dawkins told Hill he was wrong. Dawkins said that he, Grant Hill, was the best player on the team.

Hill excelled in the classroom and on the basketball court as well as in life in general. One of the main stabilizing factors in his life during that period was Coach Krzyzewski. The two would spend a lot of time talking about anything, not just basketball. Krzyzewski is regarded as one of the most honest and honorable men in college basketball, a business in which honesty is not always the priority.

"I could talk for hours about how much Coach 'K' taught me," Hill said. "He taught me about basketball. But he also taught me something more important—how to handle yourself and whatever success you may have."

Just a few short weeks into the season, Hill earned a starting position on the team. It is very rare for a college freshman to start any games for his team. As a freshman,

Grant Hill goes up against Detlef Schrempf (left), a former NBA Sixth Man of the Year Award winner. As a freshman at Duke University, Grant Hill was asked to be the basketball team's sixth man, or first player off the bench.

Grant Hill started 31 games and helped lead the Blue Devils to an NCAA berth and deep into the tournament.

Duke made it to the final four with an exciting 79–77 victory over one of their fiercest rivals, St. John's University. Then Hill made a key assist down the stretch in a win against the University of Las Vegas to clinch a championship berth. Next the Blue Devils faced off against the dangerous Kansas Jayhawks. Led by Hurley, Laettner, and Hill, the Blue Devils seized their first-ever championship with an easy 72–65 victory.

Grant Hill, a champion in his first college year, was named to the Freshman All-America team. But more important, he was now a winner and had earned the reputation of being a big-game player.

Ever the team player, Hill gave all the credit to his teammates and, of course, Coach Krzyzewski. "Coach 'K' gave a locker room speech for every game," Grant said. "And after his speech, you were ready to go out there and dive through a wall, you know?"

In his sophomore season, Hill showed the world just how versatile he could be. He was six-foot eight-inches tall. That meant he could just about play any position on the court except for center. Hill was a natural swingman. That meant he could play shooting guard or small forward, two very similar positions. But a few weeks into his sophomore year, starting point guard Bobby Hurley went down with an injury. It was nothing serious, but Hurley would miss about two weeks' worth of games.

Krzyzewski immediately moved Hill to the starting point guard position—and the team did not miss a beat. Hill started five games at point guard and the Blue Devils won all five games—including a tough 77–67 win against Louisiana State University and its star center, Shaquille O'Neal. During those games Hill averaged 16.4 points a game and 5.6 assists.

Christian Laettner (left), then with the Atlanta Hawks, watches as Grant Hill lays the ball in the basket. Laettner, Hill, and point guard Bobby Hurley led the Duke Blue Devils to their first national championship in 1991.

Hill did not make his mark that season merely with good statistics. He made his mark in pressure situations, in big games. For example, during the Atlantic Coast Conference (ACC) title game against the University of North Carolina, Hill came off the bench and shot a perfect eight-for-eight from the field and added 4 free throws for 20 points. Duke won the game, 94–74. In the NCAA regional finals against a powerhouse Kentucky team, he scored 11 points and 10 pulled down rebounds. However, no statistic was as important as his seventh assist.

With time winding down in overtime, Kentucky scored a bucket, giving them a 103–102 lead and what seemed to be a sure win. But Grant Hill inbounded the ball with an incredible court-length pass to teammate Laettner, who sank an eighteen-foot jumper at the buzzer, giving Duke another Final Four berth.

Duke became the first team to win back-to-back titles in nearly twenty years when they breezed by Michigan, 71–51, in the final. Michigan had such future NBA stars on the team as Juwan Howard, Chris Webber, and Jalen Rose. In the final game, Hill scored 18 points, snared 10 rebounds, and recorded 5 assists, 3 steals, and 2 blocked shots. Krzyzewski credited Hill with being the best player on the court. In fact, he went even further. "Grant Hill is the best player I ever coached, period," Krzyzewski would say after Hill's four years. "But he's the reluctant superstar. He wants to be the best but he doesn't separate himself from the team."

Throughout Hill's junior year, 1992–93, he was constantly being called a potential lottery pick (a very high NBA draft pick), and the all-around best player in college ball. During the summer before his junior season, Hill had a chance to play against the United States Dream Team. This squad, made up of some of the NBA's best players, practiced against college players in order to get ready for

Hill's former college coach, Mike Krzyzewski has often referred to him as the best player he has ever coached.

the Olympics. Hill learned a lot by playing against them. He learned how to be even more aggressive and to toughen up his game. He realized that he had to get even more serious about off-season workouts.

Hill hit the weight room that summer and fall to improve his strength and endurance. He also worked hard on developing more range on his outside jump shot. He entered his junior year raring to go. He led the team in scoring at 18.0 points per game and was given the Henry Iba Corinthian Award as the nation's top defender. Not only was he a total team player who could seemingly score at will, but he also was capable of stopping just about any college player in the land. But Duke had an early exit from the NCAA tournament when Jason Kidd and the California Golden Bears pulled off a stunning upset.

During his 1993–94 senior year, Hill further showed the nation and opponents what a great player and leader he was. Hill's hard work during the off-season also paid off. He had developed a nice touch on his outside jump shot. He connected on 39 three-point buckets after making only five during his first three years. Once again, Duke made it to the NCAA Tournament and Hill was named Most Valuable Player of the Southeast Regional teams. He tallied 69 points, 30 rebounds, and 23 assists in the four games.

In the third game of the tournament, Duke came out flat against a highly motivated and underdog Marquette team. Marquette trapped and pressed Duke, which had trouble bringing the ball upcourt and scoring. Hill himself was having a hard time getting his game together. At halftime, he decided that this was his last chance at another college championship game. He needed to score points, and his team needed to as well.

Grant Hill came out for the second half and started playing more aggressively. He started attacking the basket.

In the 1994 NCAA Tournament, Grant Hill went head-to-head with Glenn Robinson of the Purdue Boilermakers. Here, they meet again at the pro level.

It paid immediate dividends as he laid in the first four points of the half on beautiful baseline drives. A few minutes later, Hill showed his elevation by hitting a series of pull-up jump shots over the outstretched hands of his defender. Hill scored an incredible 16 points in the second half. Duke won, 59–49.

Then Duke was set to face the Purdue Boilermakers in the Southeast Regional semifinal game. Hill held the nation's leading scorer, Glenn "Big Dog" Robinson, to only 13 total points. Once again, Duke came out on top, 69–60.

Duke made it all the way to the final game again. But this time the University of Arkansas was too tough. They edged Grant Hill and his teammates, 76–72.

Hill, who was now ready for life in the NBA, was named an All-American, a high honor bestowed on college athletes. But Grant did more than just shine on the basketball court. He volunteered for the Read with the Blue Devils literacy program, a program designed to encourage youngsters to read. In 1993 he served as the cochairperson of Durham's Project Graduation. This was a program that promoted a drug-and alcohol-free graduation party for high school students.

Grant graduated with honors and a major in history. Then he waited anxiously to see which NBA team would draft him.

Chapter 5

A Great Beginning

The Detroit Pistons, who only five years before had celebrated a world championship, had fallen on hard times by 1994. Gone were reliable superstars like Isiah Thomas and Bill Laimbeer. The only remaining star from the championship years of the mid 1980s was shooting guard Joe Dumars.

In 1993–94, while Hill was a senior at Duke, the Pistons were mired in their worst season ever. The team lost a club-record 62 games and saw no relief in sight—except for one thing. Because of their poor record, the Pistons held the third pick in the draft. This meant they were guaranteed to get one of the top college players. But it was clear from the start that the Pistons wanted only one player: Grant Hill.

The Pistons were sure that Grant Hill, the player, could become an NBA superstar. They felt that his talent and versatility made him the kind of player a team could build around. But the Pistons wanted to make sure that Grant Hill, the person, would be a superstar too. So the team called Hill and asked him to come for an interview.

"He was impressive in every way," said Billy McKinney, former vice president of the team. "He spoke so well. He listened well and knew so much about the history of our organization. It was like he studied up on us."

Hill walked away from the interview positive about one thing: He wanted to play for the Pistons just as much as the Pistons wanted him. The only problem was that there were two teams that would pick players before the Pistons: the Milwaukee Bucks and the Dallas Mavericks. Predraft rumors indicated that the Bucks were set to take the NCAA's leading scorer, Glenn Robinson. But nobody really knew how the Mavericks were going to pick. There was even talk of Detroit trading its draft pick away if Dallas decided to choose Hill.

Head Coach Don Chaney paced around nervously as the Mavericks hesitated before making their selection. They wound up choosing point guard Jason Kidd, meaning Hill would go to the Pistons.

Grant Hill was now an NBA player. McKinney was so happy that he actually burst into tears. "We've talked a lot about the kinds of people we want to acquire to help us get back to the top," McKinney said. "I had a little formula— TCTP. Talent, Character, and a Team Player. Grant Hill embodies that phrase. He's a professional."

Hill grew up in a wealthy environment, but the Pistons soon made him an extremely rich man. They signed Hill to an eight-year contract worth about $45 million. Now the only thing left was to play.

From the minute Hill stepped on the basketball court with his new teammates, it was clear that he belonged in the NBA. He was able to weave in and out of defenses, always knew where and when to expect the ball, and also knew where his teammates would be positioned.

Chaney, who had previously played in the NBA, said that Hill reminded him of former Celtics great Larry Bird. He said the two players shared a court sense, a complete understanding of the game.

Putting the ball on the floor, Grant Hill looks to dribble past Kevin Garnett. Detroit used the third-overall pick in the 1994 NBA Draft to take Hill.

Joe Dumars was immediately impressed by the rookie. "The guy's never out of position on the court," Dumars said. "Never."

Hill had a very impressive rookie season. He led the Pistons in scoring, with an average of 19.9 points per game, and led them in steals with 1.77 per game. He also averaged 6.4 rebounds a game and an even 5 assists. Those statistics prove that Hill is a very active player. It means that he is not content with only scoring points. He plays defense, passes, and rebounds the ball.

Hill was becoming well known outside of Detroit as well. In fact, basketball fans throughout the country voted Hill in as a starter for the Eastern Conference team in the annual NBA All-Star Game. He became the first rookie ever to lead all players in fan voting. Hill admitted to being a little nervous before the game, since he was playing with and against the great players he had idolized and analyzed on his videotapes. But he did very well. Hill was stingy with his shots, but he made five out of eight, scoring 10 points.

The All-Star Game also seemed to catapult Hill to a higher level of play after the break. On March 25, at home against a weak Boston Celtics team, he exploded for 33 points and 16 rebounds. He would match the 33-point mark two more times before the season was over. Then on April 7, Hill notched the first triple-double of his career. The most common triple-double occurs when a player scores ten or more points, grabs ten or more rebounds, and passes for ten or more assists. Getting ten steals or blocked shots could also help earn a player a triple-double. Hill accomplished this tough feat against the Orlando Magic when he scored 21, had 11 rebounds, and handed out 10 assists during a Pistons victory.

Soon Grant Hill's face was on the cover of all the major sports magazines. One article even boldly said he would save sports in America. Hill was not comfortable with all

During the 1994–95 season, Hill became the first rookie to lead all players in fan voting to the All-Star Game. He also led his team in scoring and assists.

the attention, especially with the talk of him being the next Michael Jordan. But Hill had to learn to adapt. This is where having a former professional athlete for a father helped out. "In my rookie year, I had to adjust," Hill said. "All of a sudden you're in the NBA, you're on your own, you have a lot of money and on top of that the celebrity status is thrust on you. It may not sound like it but it was difficult. Having a father who has been there and could share with me, helped me out a great deal."

There is one thing that Grant Hill did not like doing as a rookie, and still does not like: signing autographs. He does sign them and tries to accommodate fans whenever he can, but it is something he does not enjoy. He has a good reason.

"The reason why, I guess, is when I was little and was out with my dad," Hill said. "When we were out in public, being in a restaurant, after a football game, and people coming up and wanting my dad's autograph—it was kind of taking time away from me. So I never quite understood the significance of autographs."

Hill went on to win the Rookie of the Year Award. He was actually the cowinner in a tie with Jason Kidd. Unfortunately, Hill was unable to turn the Pistons around in a single season. After finishing 20–62 before he got there, the Pistons improved slightly to 28–54 with him. But the team was confident that with Grant Hill as the nucleus, it was finally on the right track.

Hill's athleticism amazed Chaney every time he watched Hill play. "He has the most perfect body I've ever seen," Chaney said. "He's perfectly proportioned and athletically pure, and it makes him the most deceiving player in the world."

Hill was unusually mature for such a young man. He credits his parents and family and friends with helping him adjust. It is obvious that he has a good head on his

Most observers are impressed with Hill's athleticism.

shoulders and knows what is expected of him. He is well spoken, polite, and educated. He firmly believes that an athlete should give back to the community where he or she stars.

That is why right after Hill won the Rookie of the Year Award, he started the Grant Hill Summer Basketball Program, which offers instruction in basketball and academics to inner-city children in Detroit. That is only one of the many charitable programs that Hill has undertaken. "I think it's neat being a role model," Hill said. "I like being in a position where I can have a positive effect on people. Hopefully, I'll do a good job."

Grant Hill, with one solid NBA season under his belt, was ready to do a good job in year number two.

Chapter 6

Franchise Player

In just his second year of professional basketball, Grant Hill continued to make history. He became only the fifteenth player in the history of the NBA to lead his team in scoring, rebounding, and assists in the same season. He also led the team in steals and minutes played.

He finished the campaign with averages of 20.2 points, 9.8 rebounds, and 6.9 assists per game. He was also once again the leading vote-getter for the NBA All-Star Game. This time, a more relaxed Hill scored 14 points in the mid-season classic.

Doug Collins, a former NBA All-Star himself, was the new head coach of the Pistons. He brought a fiery, intense style to the young team that seemed to motivate them immediately. Together with Hill, they led the team to a playoff berth—only two years after losing more than sixty games and only one year after losing fifty games.

The Pistons were swept in three straight games by the tough Orlando Magic, but it did not matter to Detroit's fans. They were just happy that their team was back again in contention. Hill was the leading scorer of the series for Detroit, averaging 19.0 points a game.

After the season, another wish came true for Hill. He played for the United States in the 1996 Olympic Games in

Atlanta, Georgia. Grant Hill, college standout, NBA All-Star, was now a member of the Dream Team. Hill was no stranger to international competition, however. He played in the World Junior Championships in 1990, and in 1991 he competed in the Pan American Games in Cuba.

Ever since the United States started sending NBA players to the Olympics in 1992, there has been some concern about the integrity of the games. Critics say that the NBA players are too good and that they are destroying any chance of competition. Hill and his teammates, which included superstars Karl Malone and Hakeem Olajuwon, cruised through most of the challengers. They faced a tough Yugoslavian team but still managed to win the gold medal, winning the final game, 95–69.

"We may have blown out most of the competition but we still had our hands full against Yugoslavia in the gold medal game," Hill said. "The rest of the world sends their best players, so it makes sense for the United States to send their best."

Grant Hill was now a bona fide superstar, known throughout the world, but he did not rest on his laurels. Hill wanted to get even better, and he wanted to help bring a championship to Detroit.

As usual, Hill, who loves to listen to rhythm and blues music and loves the group Earth Wind and Fire, also kept busy off the court. He had numerous endorsement deals with the likes of FILA, McDonald's, and Sprite, among others, and he got involved in charitable programs more than ever.

Hill has served on the Special Olympics board of directors, served senior citizens Christmas meals with the Meals on Wheels program, is involved with refurbishing parks throughout Detroit, donates FILA shoes to underprivileged children throughout the world, and also donates lots

Grant Hill's immense talents earned him a spot on the 1996 U.S. Olympic Men's Basketball Team after only his second season of pro ball. The Americans won the gold medal, beating Yugoslavia in the final game.

of money to Covenant House and the YWCA Coalition for Homeless Children and Families.

During the 1996–97 season, Hill continued to build on what is sure to be a spectacular career. He averaged 21.4 points per game as he improved his shooting accuracy to a career-high .496. That meant that Hill made almost half the shots he attempted. He was voted the NBA Player of the Month for January. But that season Hill saved the best for last. He led the league with 13 triple-doubles, including six in his final eleven games of the season! The last game of the regular season was against Detroit's toughest rival, the Indiana Pacers. Even though both teams had clinched play-off berths, both wanted to end the season on a winning note. Hill and Indiana superstar Reggie Miller traded baskets all game long. But it was Hill who caught fire in overtime, nailing a big three-pointer down the stretch to seal a 124–120 game. He finished with 38 points.

The Pistons had another quick exit from the playoffs. Detroit was ousted by Atlanta in five games. Hill averaged better than 23 points a game for the series. After the season, he was selected to the All-NBA first team.

The next season, 1997–98, was something of a disappointment for Hill and the Pistons. Coach Collins and his tough, sometimes abrasive, style had worn thin with some of the veterans. They said that he was too hard on the team and that he was constantly putting them down. Pistons management heard the rumblings but allowed Collins to stay. Unfortunately, Collins traded away a good bulk of the team. He sent veterans like Otis Thorpe, Terry Mills, Michael Curry, Theo Ratliff, and Aaron McKie away. This bunch was very tough and contributed to the aggressive style of play that had led the Pistons to 54 wins the previous season. He brought in talented but less physical players such as Jerry Stackhouse, Brian Williams (later known as Bison Dele), and Malik Sealy.

Beating his man, Grant Hill gets by Kobe Bryant of the Lakers. Hill and Bryant are both exciting NBA players.

The result was disastrous. The Pistons muddled through a terrible season. Even though Hill's statistics were similar to those of years past, he seemed to lose his usual zeal for the game. In fact, Hill was so tired of Collins's overbearing manner that he missed one game with the flu and was not enjoying himself. "It was the first time in my life that I didn't feel like playing," he said. "I can't lie. It crossed my mind that maybe I could get hurt and be out the rest of the year."

The situation got worse, and management finally fired Doug Collins. They appointed as the new head coach Assistant Coach Alvin Gentry, who was more easygoing and was well liked by the players.

Hill was hurt. A lot of people were starting to blame him for the Pistons' inability to advance in the playoffs. He was getting frustrated. In any sport, but particularly in basketball, it is very hard to win with only one great player on a team. Even the Chicago Bulls' Michael Jordan had Scottie Pippen and Dennis Rodman—two potential Hall of Famers—as his teammates.

Hill responded to the criticism as he does to almost everything else in life: He looked at it as a learning experience. "I'm really glad I've gone through this because I learned a lot about myself," he said. "I have a new focus on basketball and life. I learned what I need to do."

Grant Hill was rejuvenated and went back to playing the brand of basketball his fans expected. He started taking more of the brunt of the team on his shoulders. This was Grant Hill's team now, and he did not disappoint, although the team failed to make the playoffs. In fact, the better the competition was, the better he played.

"Scottie Pippen is my favorite player to play against," Hill said. "I don't necessarily do well against him. He's the best at my position and it's always a challenge to go against him. He was on a championship team and he's a versatile player. He is where I'd like to get someday."

The 1998–99 season was shortened due to a labor dispute between players and the owners. The season started in January and teams wound up playing only fifty games (A regular season is eighty-two games.) It was an up-and-down season for the Pistons. They started off with three victories but then promptly lost the next five games. They then won 9 of 12 before dropping three straight. It was a hard season for them and for Coach Gentry, who was in his first full season as head coach.

Even though the team fluctuated, Grant Hill, as usual, was the mainstay. For the third time in four seasons Hill led the team in scoring, rebounding, and assists. He is only the fourth player in NBA history to lead his team in all three of those categories more than once. The other three are Hall of Famers: Elgin Baylor, Wilt Chamberlain, and Larry Bird. Even though he has only played professionally for five seasons, Hill's name certainly belongs among the greats.

The Orlando Magic, who recently have had topflight players such as Shaquille O'Neal and Penny Hardaway leave the team, spent the summer of 2000 adding some real star power to the franchise.

In August, the Magic executed a sign and trade agreement with the Pistons that landed them Grant Hill. After Hill had signed a new contract, the Pistons traded him for Chucky Atkins and Ben Wallace. Hill was interested in moving to a warmer climate, but also wanted to join a franchise he felt was committed to winning. Hill felt the Magic, who also added Tracy McGrady during the off-season, were in a better position to win a championship than the Pistons were.

"I was a big fan of theirs, and I kind of felt that if I were to leave Detroit, this is where I wanted to go," Hill said

After the 1998–99 season, Hill hired a coach to work with him on improving his jump shot. Although he was already one of the best players in the league, he still wanted to improve.

about joining the Magic. "What was really impressive, and I'm not sure if I should say this, is Horace Grant had good things to say and he's a guy who got traded."

As the 2000–01 season got underway, Hill was still hobbled by an ankle injury he sustained at the end of the 1999–00 season. Though he tried his best to play through the pain, he decided to have season ending ankle surgery. He appeared in just 4 games.

Grant Hill is not one to rest on his laurels. He has never been satisfied with his personal statistics or personal fame. Hill wants to be part of a winning tradition. "I think I will have a great career in the sense that I will have done a lot and accomplished a lot," Hill said. "But I think having a ring—having a championship—puts you in a different class. I want to be remembered as a great player who won a championship, who won a lot of championships."

Something just as important for Hill is his loyalty to the fans. While he avoids comparisons to Michael Jordan, Hill realizes that with Jordan gone, somebody will have to make sure the NBA remains the positive force that people like Larry Bird, Magic Johnson, and Michael Jordan helped create.

Hill, with his arcing jump shot, thunderous slam dunks, and tenacious defense, is up to the task. Along with other young superstars such as Jason Kidd, Kobe Bryant, Tim Duncan, Vince Carter, and Allen Iverson, he represents the basketball stars, the future of the NBA as it begins the twenty-first century.

"We have a huge responsibility," Hill said, "me and some of the other young guys, to help carry the NBA and do some of the things for the NBA that previous guys have done. It's a huge responsibility, but I think we can do it."

Career Statistics

COLLEGE

YEAR	TEAM	GP	FG%	REB	PTS	AVG
1990–91	Duke	36	.516	185	402	11.2
1991–92	Duke	33	.611	187	463	14.0
1992–93	Duke	26	.578	166	468	18.0
1993–94	Duke	34	.462	233	591	17.4
Totals		129	.532	771	1,924	14.9

NBA

YEAR	TEAM	GP	FG%	REB	AST	STL	BLK	PTS	RPG	PPG
1994–95	Detroit	70	.477	445	353	124	62	1,394	6.4	19.9
1995–96	Detroit	80	.462	783	548	100	48	1,618	9.8	20.2
1996–97	Detroit	80	.496	721	583	144	48	1,710	9.0	21.4
1997–98	Detroit	81	.452	623	551	143	53	1,712	7.7	21.1
1998–99	Detroit	50	.479	355	300	80	27	1,053	7.1	21.1
1999–00	Detroit	74	.489	490	385	103	43	1,906	6.6	25.8
2000–01	Orlando	4	.442	25	25	5	2	55	6.3	13.8
Totals		439	.476	3,442	2,745	699	283	9,448	7.8	21.5

GP=Games Played
FG%=Field Goal Percentage
REB=Rebounds

AST=Assists
STL=Steals
BLK=Blocks

PTS=Points scored
RPG=Rebounds per game
PPG=Points per game

Where to Write Grant Hill

Mr. Grant Hill
c/o Orlando Magic
Orlando Arena
One Magic Place
Orlando, FL 32801

Internet Addresses

http://www.nba.com/playerfile/grant_hill.html
http://espn.go.com/nba/profiles/profile/2626.html

Index